My First Animal Library
Rhinoceroses
by Penelope S. Nelson

Bullfrog Books

Ideas for Parents and Teachers

Bullfrog Books let children practice reading informational text at the earliest reading levels. Repetition, familiar words, and photo labels support early readers.

Before Reading

- Discuss the cover photo. What does it tell them?

- Look at the picture glossary together. Read and discuss the words.

Read the Book

- "Walk" through the book and look at the photos. Let the child ask questions. Point out the photo labels.

- Read the book to the child, or have him or her read independently.

After Reading

- Prompt the child to think more. Ask: What did you know about rhinoceroses before reading this book? What more would you like to learn about them after reading it?

Bullfrog Books are published by Jump!
5357 Penn Avenue South
Minneapolis, MN 55419
www.jumplibrary.com

Library of Congress Cataloging-in-Publication Data

Names: Nelson, Penelope, 1994– author.
Title: Rhinoceroses / by Penelope S. Nelson.
Description: Bullfrog books edition.
Minneapolis, MN : Jump!, Inc., [2020]
Series: My first animal library
Audience: Age 5–8. | Audience: K to Grade 3.
Includes bibliographical references and index.
Identifiers: LCCN 2018039529 (print)
LCCN 2018040674 (ebook)
ISBN 9781641285636 (ebook)
ISBN 9781641285629 (hardcover : alk. paper)
Subjects: LCSH: Rhinoceroses—Juvenile literature.
Classification: LCC QL737.U63 (ebook)
LCC QL737.U63 N46 2020 (print)
DDC 599.66/8—dc23
LC record available at https://lccn.loc.gov/2018039529

Editor: Jenna Trnka
Designer: Jenna Casura

Photo Credits: Aaron Amat/Shutterstock, cover; rusm/iStock, 1; Eric Isselee/Shutterstock, 3; imageBROKER/Alamy, 4, 16; Corrie Barnard/Shutterstock, 5, 23tr; double-P/iStock, 6–7, 23bl; THPStock/Shutterstock, 8–9; kamchatka/Age Fotostock, 10–11; Theo Allofs/Minden Pictures/SuperStock, 12; robertharding/SuperStock, 13; Alfredo Garcia Saz/Shutterstock, 14–15; Zoonar GmbH/Alamy, 17; James Hager/Getty, 18; 2630ben/iStock, 18–19; Hugo Alonso/Age Fotostock, 20–21, 23tl; Anan Kaewkhammul/Shutterstock, 22; digitalg/iStock, 23br; irakite/iStock, 24.

Printed in the United States of America at Corporate Graphics in North Mankato, Minnesota.

Table of Contents

Charge!

This is a rhinoceros.

We call it a rhino.

It charges!
Why?
It is scared.
It leads with
its horns.

5

It is safe.

It grazes on grass.

Rhinos live in dry areas.

Most live alone.

They like to have space.

They love mud.

Why?

The sun is hot.

Mud keeps them cool.

This rhino has one horn.

horn

This rhino has two.

horns

Rhinos are heavy.

How heavy?

Heavier than a car!

oxpecker

Oxpeckers sit on them.

These birds help.

How?

They eat parasites off of the rhinos.

Nice!

The birds call.
Something is near!
Charge!

Moms have one calf at a time.

It will grow big!

calf

Parts of a Rhinoceros

ears
Rhinos have great hearing to listen for danger.

eyes
Rhinos have poor eyesight. Sometimes they charge at trees, thinking they are a threat!

horns
Rhinos charge and lead with their horns. The horns are made from the same material as human fingernails!

skin
Rhino skin is thick and often makes folds.

nose
Rhinos have a good sense of smell. It helps them know what is around them, especially since they cannot see well.

Picture Glossary

calf
A baby rhino.

charges
Attacks in a rush.

grazes
Feeds on growing plants.

parasites
Animals or plants that live on or in another animal or plant.

Index

To Learn More

Finding more information is as easy as 1, 2, 3.

❶ Go to www.factsurfer.com

❷ Enter "rhinoceroses" into the search box.

❸ Click the "Surf" button to see a list of websites.